Lots of Rabbits to Spot

Written by Louie Stowell

Illustrated by David Semple

Designed by Matthew Bromley,
Laura Nelson, Helen Lee
and Vicky Barker

Edited by Anna Milbourne

Look at all the places you can find in this book. I'm so excited about Bunnyfest!

Visit the rabbits in their burrows on pages 4-5.

It's time for school on pages 6-7.

There's a bustling market on pages 8-9.

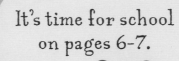

See racing rabbits at the Rabbit Olympics on pages 14-15.

Everyone's invited to Princess Beatrix's birthday party on pages 10-11.

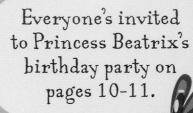

Spend a night under the stars on pages 12-13.

Shh! The play has already begun on pages 16-17.

The rabbits are relaxing in a glade on pages 18-19.

Visit the Rabbit History Museum on pages 20-21.

It's festival time on pages 22-23. Get ready to rock at Bunnyfest!

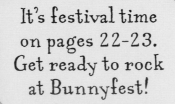

You'll find lots of games and puzzles on pages 24-30, and answers on pages 31-32.

Here are some friendly rabbits you'll see in every scene... and one sly fox who's a pesky pest.

Chef Hopkins cooks everything from carrot cakes to lettuce pie.

Professor McDigger loves to dig up ancient objects.

Becca Bucktooth is a motorcycle-riding daredevil.

Bob Cottontail is a helpful repair rabbit.

WATCH OUT, TWITCH!

Skip and Twitch are twins but they're not alike at all. Skip is very sensible but Twitch loves taking risks.

Old Nana Rabbit always has her knitting close at hand.

The Velveteen Underground

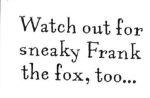

Eat your carrots to keep your eyes sharp. The Velveteen Underground, a rabbit rock band, is somewhere in every scene.

Watch out for sneaky Frank the fox, too...

How many of each of these things can you spot?

Rabbits with trowels

Toy bunnies

Sleeping teachers

Red clocks

Rabbits playing recorders

To the market

How many carrots are there on this table?

There is no such thing as a silly question.

Eat your 5 carrots a day.

Run, Rabbits, RUN!

Can you count eight bushes with purple berries?

6

How many of each of these can you find?

Delivery rabbits

Baskets of strawberries

Bunches of purple carrots

Carrot cakes

Lettuce juice sellers

How many boxes of carrots are in this pile?

Where can I decorate some eggs?

Can you spot each of these things?

Court jester

Magician

Painting of the queen

Blue bunny balloon

Gigantic diamond

Can you spot my other shoe? I lost it when I was dancing.

Cloakroom

THAT MUST BE WORTH A MILLION CARROTS!

HAPPY BIRTHDAY, BEATRIX!

Where is the palace servant who is pouring tea?

Can you spot each of these things?

Rabbit on a night hike

Wide-eyed owl

Camper van

Shadow rabbit

Grumpy, sleepy rabbit

Who has some tools and can help me put up my tent?

GRR!

THANKS, BOB!

To find my tent, follow the trail of carrots...

PUZZLES AND GAMES

You'll find stickers to use in these puzzles and games at the back of the book.

Match the cake stickers to these shapes.

CAKES

Each rabbit started off with five carrots. Who's eaten the most?

Time's up! Stick a ribbon next to the winner.

CARROT-EATING COMPETITION

Connect the dots to finish this picture.

Use the stickers to build a bunny totem pole.

The finished totem pole will look like this.

Use the stickers to pack me a lunch exactly like Skip's.

Twitch's lunchbox

Skip's lunchbox

Use the stickers to give each rabbit the right scoops of ice cream.

1 scoop carrot
2 scoops pink radish

3 scoops lettuce
1 scoop carrot

1 scoop lettuce
1 scoop pink radish
1 scoop carrot

Can you spot 11 differences between these two market stalls?

If Twitch and Skip pick every purple berry they pass, who will have more by the time they reach the toadstools?

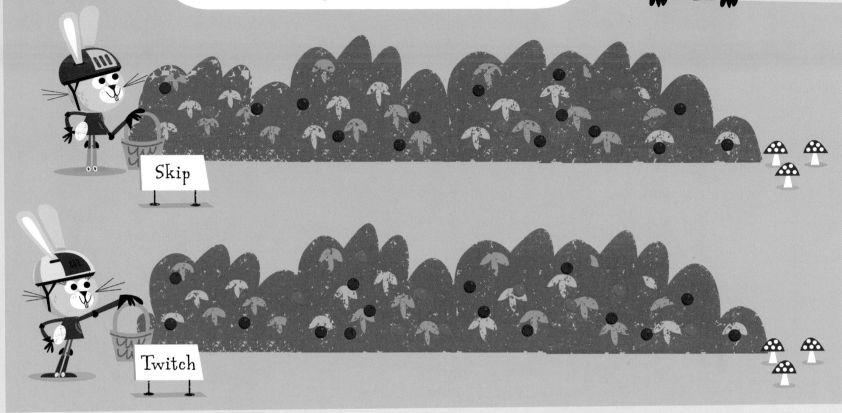

Skip

Twitch

This Golden Carrot was made by rabbits long ago. There are 10 more hidden throughout this book. Can you help me find them all?

The carrots look like this.

Use the stickers to put my motorcycle together and then add my boots, gloves, helmet and cape.

Follow the order on the sticker pages.

Help Twitch finish her picture by filling it in with pencils or felt-tip pens.

Answers

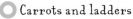
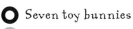

4-5

- Lettuce cushion
- Mailrabbit
- Carrots and ladders
- Grow-your-own carrots

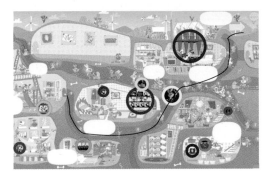

- Chef is growing four giant carrots.

- 〜 Way to school
- Becca has six crash helmets
- Orange bag
- Magnifying glass
- Nana has a pet worm.
- Nana's grandson

6-7

- Four rabbits with trowels
- One sleeping teacher
- Seven toy bunnies
- Two red clocks

Differences between pictures

- Five rabbits playing recorders
- Bushes with purple berries
- Green watering can
- Six carrots on the table
- Music lesson

8-9

- Three delivery rabbits
- Eight bunches of purple carrots
- Five lettuce juice sellers
- Seven baskets of strawberries
- Nine carrot cakes
- Five boxes of carrots

- Purple basket
- Rabbit with a tall cake
- Becca is above the market.
- Egg decoration
- Book stall

10-11

- Court jester
- Painting of the queen
- Gigantic diamond
- Magician
- Blue bunny balloon
- Lost shoe

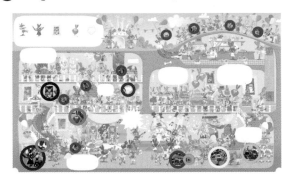

- Servant pouring tea
- Friend in the same dress
- Green presents
- Empty chair

12-13

- Rabbit on a night hike
- Camper van
- Wide-eyed owl
- Shadow rabbit

- Grumpy, sleepy rabbit
- Tent at the end of the trail
- Chef is cooking vegetables.
- Bob can help put up a tent.
- Unlit bonfire
- Five rabbits are waving flags.

14-15

- Four carrot bikes
- Seven hurdle racers
- Nine volunteers
- 10 flags

- Nana is knitting a crash mat.
- Eight other rabbits wearing mascot costumes
- Royal family
- T-shirts on sale here
- Other runner in blue
- Six rabbits in the pyramid

16-17

- ○ Rabbit carrying scenery
- ○ Box of face paints
- ○ Sleeping rabbit
- ○ Orange fairy-rabbit

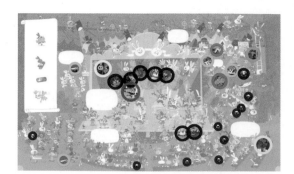

- ○ Blue wig
- ● Seven masked dancers
- ● Red boxes of popcorn
- ○ Four more swords
- ○ Becca is in the spotlight.

18-19

- ● Five toy shovels
- ○ 10 purple chairs
- ○ Eight rabbits with carrot ice creams
- ○ Three life rings

- ○ Tree house
- ○ Daisy-chain friends
- ● Seven paper boats
- ○ Professor McDigger has found a vase.
- ● This kite belongs to the rabbit asking the question.

20-21

- ○ Cave-rabbit painting
- ● Painting of an old car
- ● Jewel-studded sword
- ○ Spiked helmet

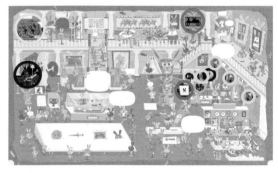

Differences between the statues

- ● This is where rabbits can try on helmets.
- ● Bob is fixing a statue.
- ○ Axes

22-23

- ○ 10 carrot burgers
- ○ Nine festival hats
- ● Five rabbits on stilts
- ○ Two one-rabbit bands

- ○ Hot-air balloon
- ○ Becca is leaping over seven logs.
- ● Rainbow arches
- ○ Chef is judging the contest.
- ● Puppet show

Games

Cakes matched to their shapes

Ice creams for each rabbit

Competition winner. He's eaten four carrots.

It's a carrot mascot from the Olympics.

Skip will have more purple berries.

Differences between the two stalls

This is what Becca and her motorcycle should look like.

Stick these cakes onto the matching shapes on Chef's cake stand.

    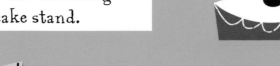 

Who won the carrot-eating competition?

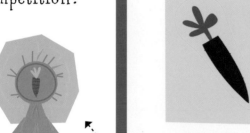

Stick this ribbon next to the winner.

Use these stickers to pack a lunch for Twitch that matches Skip's on page 25. Use the spare stickers anywhere you like.

Stick all these stickers onto the bunny totem pole on page 25. Follow the numbers here to stick each piece in the right order.

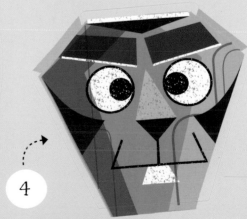

5

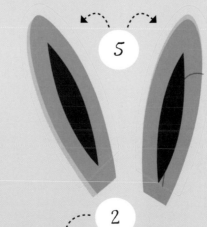

4

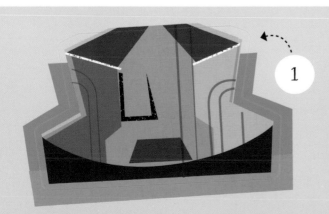

1

2

3

Use these stickers on pages 26-27.

Stick us next to our bandmates.

Where can I do a stunt on my unicycle?

I'm judging the giant vegetable competition.

Stick us on the skate ramp.

Put me wherever you like you.

Match these stickers to the right stalls.

Egg Painting

Nana's Knits

Bob's Bikes

Juicy Drinks

Put these on the white tables, for Chef to judge in the Giant Vegetable Competition.

Boing! Stick us bouncing around on the trampolines, please.

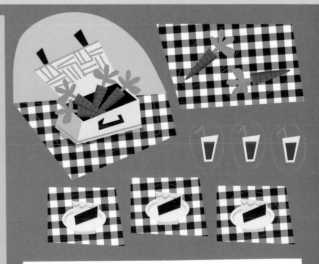

Give the rabbits who are sitting on the red and white picnic blanket some food and drinks.

Add this magician to the scene and give him an audience.

Give these balloons and this kite to the rabbits who are asking for them.

Add these stickers to the scene on pages 26-27 to show more rabbits having fun.

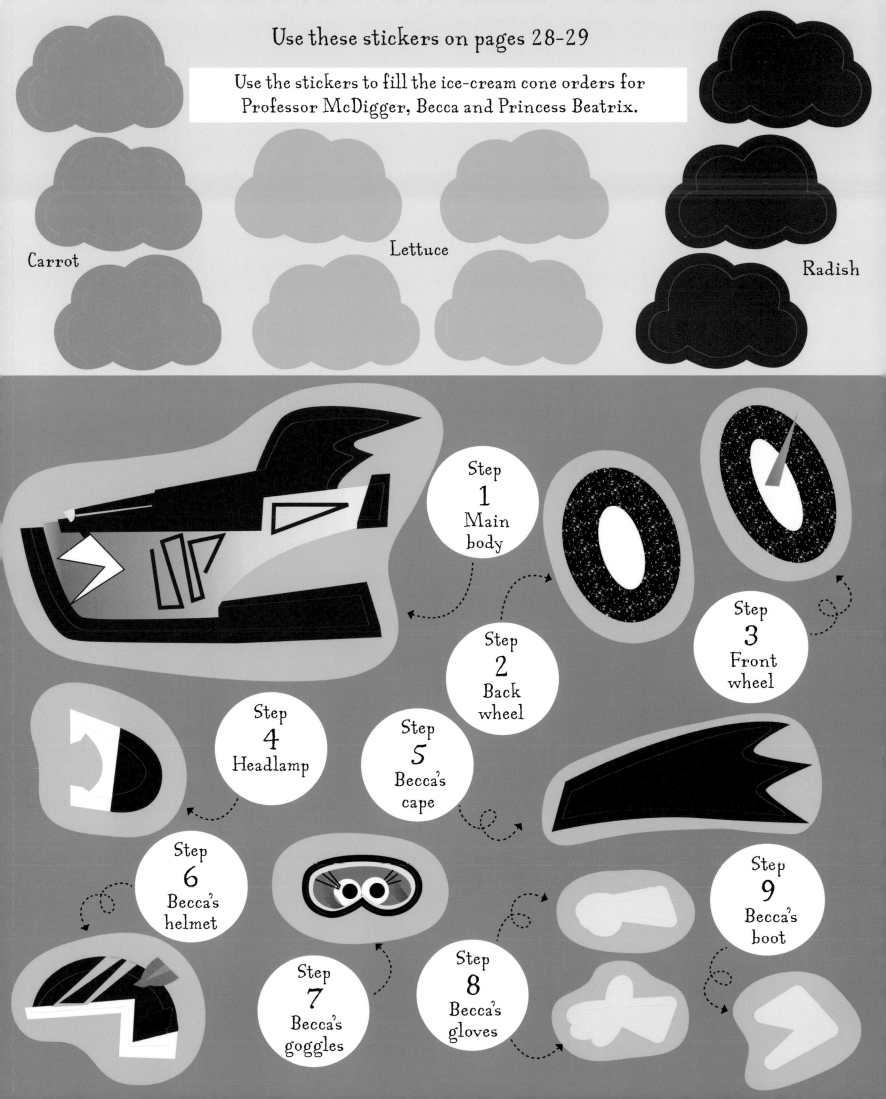